Fucking Games

Grae Cleugh

Methuen Drama

Published by Methuen 2001

1 3 5 7 9 10 8 6 4 2

First published in 2001 by
Methuen Publishing Limited,
215 Vauxhall Bridge Road, London SW1V 1EJ

Methuen Publishing Limited Reg. No. 3543167

A CIP catalogue record for this book is available from the British Library

ISBN 0 413 77195 4

Typeset by SX Composing DTP, Rayleigh, Essex
Printed and bound in Great Britain by
Cox & Wyman Ltd, Reading, Berkshire

ROYAL COURT

Royal Court Theatre presents

FUCKING GAMES

by **Grae Cleugh**

First performance at the Royal Court Jerwood Theatre Upstairs
Sloane Square, London on 8 November 2001.

Supported by Jerwood New Playwrights.

J ERWOOD
NEW PLAYWRIGHTS

FUCKING GAMES

by **Grae Cleugh**

Cast in order of appearance
Terence **Allan Corduner**
Jonah **Ian Dunn**
Jude **Daniel Lapaine**
Danny **Benjamin Davies**

Director **Dominic Cooke**
Designer **Christopher Oram**
Lighting Designer **Johanna Town**
Sound Designer **Ian Dickinson**
Assistant Director **Nina Raine**
Casting Director **Lisa Makin**
Production Manager **Sue Bird**
Company Stage Manager **Cath Binks**
Stage Management **Suzanne Bourke, Dani Youngman**
Costume Supervisor **Laura Hunt**
Company Voice Work **Patsy Rodenburg**
Set built by **Rupert Blakely**
Set painted by **Richard Nutborne**

Royal Court Theatre would like to thank the following for their help with this production:
V-Tech Electronics UK PLC, Mentzendorff, The Kensington Lighting Company, Watford Palace Theatre,
Wardrobe care by Persil and Comfort courtesy of Lever Fabergé.

THE COMPANY

Grae Cleugh (writer)
Fucking Games is Grae's first full-length play.
He was shortlisted for the Westminster Prize 1998
for his short play Eight, Nine, Ten Out.
He is currently studying acting at the Royal Scottish
Academy of Music and Drama.

Dominic Cooke (director)
Associate Director of the Royal Court.
For the Royal Court: Redundant, Spinning into
Butter, Fireface, Other People.
Other theatre includes: As adapter and director:
Arabian Nights (Young Vic/UK and world tour/
New Victory Theatre, New York); The Marriage
of Figaro (tour). As director: Hunting Scenes From
Lower Bavaria, The Weavers (Gate), Afore Night
Come, Entertaining Mr Sloane (Theatr Clwyd); The
Bullet (Donmar Warehouse); My Mother Said I
Never Should (Oxford Stage Company/ Young Vic);
Of Mice and Men (Nottingham Playhouse); Kiss Of
the Spiderwoman (Bolton Octagon); Autogeddon
(Edinburgh Assembly Rooms); Caravan (National
Theatre of Norway); The Importance of Being
Earnest (Atlantic Theatre Festival, Canada).
Opera includes: I Capuleti e i Montacchi (Grange
Park Opera).
Awards include: TMA Award for Arabian Nights,
Manchester Evening News Drama Award for The
Marriage of Figaro and Edinburgh Fringe First for
Autogeddon.
Assistant Director at the Royal Shakespeare
Company 1992-94.

Allan Corduner
For the Royal Court: Three Birds Alighting on a
Field, Icecream, Serious Money (Wyndhams/Public
& Royale Theater, New York).
Other theatre includes: The Heart of Art (Off-
Broadway); Titanic (Broadway); Insignificance,
Arsenic and Old Lace (Chichester); Walpurgis
Night, Salvation (Gate); Rosmersholm (Young Vic);
Marya (Old Vic); The Boys Next Door (Hampstead
& Comedy); The Beaux Stratagem (RNT);
Milkwood Blues (Lyric Studio); Now We Are Sixty
(Cambridge Festival); Amadeus, Play It Again Sam
(Thorndike, Leatherhead); A Midsummer Night's
Dream (New Shakespeare Company); Once a
Catholic (Wyndhams); Misalliance (Birmingham
Rep); Measure for Measure, The Devil is an Ass
(Edinburgh Festival & RNT); The Amazons, The
Entertainer (Actors Company).
Television includes: The Way We Live Now,
Liverpool One, Drop the Dead Donkey, Operation
Gadgetman, Mad About You, Nostromo, Love in
the Ancient World, No Bananas, An Independent
Man, Stick With Me Kid, The Bill, The Last
Machine, Nobody's Children, Birdland, Boon,
Inspector Morse, Teenage Health Freak,

Headhunters, Antonia & Jane: The Definitive
Mid-Life Report, Minder, The Dame Edna
Experience, Mandela, Freud, Diamonds,
Roots, Buccaneer.
Film includes: Food of Love, Baby's in Black,
Me Without You, The Grey Zone, The Search
for John Gissing, Kiss Kiss Bang Bang (all to be
released), Joe Gould's Secret, Gladiator, Topsy
Turvy, The Impostors, Norma and Marilyn,
Alive and Kicking, Soup, Voices From a
Locked Room, Heart of Darkness, A Business
Affair, Carry on Columbus, Edward II, Talk
Radio, Shadowmakers, Hearts of Fire, Return
of the Soldier, Bad Medicine, Yentl, Sredni
Vashtar.

Benjamin Davies
Fucking Games is Benjamin's first professional
production.
Benjamin was awarded a PMA at the Olivier
Award Bursaries 2000.

Ian Dickinson (sound designer)
For the Royal Court: Herons, Cutting
Through the Carnival.
Other theatre includes: Search and Destroy
(New End, Hampstead); Phaedra, Three
Sisters, The Shaughraun, Writer's Cramp
(Royal Lyceum, Edinburgh); The Whore's
Dream (RSC Fringe, Edinburgh); As You Like
It, An Experienced Woman Gives Advice,
Present Laughter, The Philadelphia Story,
Wolks World, Poor Superman, Martin
Yesterday, Fast Food, Coyote Ugly, Prizenight
(Royal Exchange, Manchester); Great
Monsters of Western Street (Throat Theatre
Company); Small Craft Warnings, Tieble and
Her Demon (Manchester Evening News
Theatre Awards Best Design Team), The
Merchant of Venice, Death and The Maiden
(Library Theatre Company, Manchester).
Ian is Sound Deputy at the Royal Court.

Ian Dunn
For the Royal Court: Toast, I Am Yours, Babies,
Six Degrees of Separation (& Comedy).
Other theatre includes: Luminosity, Loveplay
(RSC); Chips With Everything, Somewhere
(RNT); Our Boys (Donmar/Derby Playhouse);
A Prayer for Wings (tour); Hidden Laughter
(Vaudeville); Forget Me Not Lane (Greenwich);
Invisible Friends, Wolf at the Door, Brighton
Beach Memoirs (Scarborough).
Television includes: Peak Practice, Bad Girls,
Holby City, The Bill, Reach for the Moon, Bliss,
Stone, Sissors, Paper, Gulliver's Travels, Shine on
Harvey Moon, Casualty, Desmonds, Jackanory:
The Gulf, The Merrihill Millionaires, A Touch of
Frost, Soldier, Soldier, Children of the North,
Sweet Capital Lives.
Film includes: American Friends, Bye Bye Baby.

Daniel Lapaine
Theatre includes: Les Parents Terribles, King
Lear (Sydney Theatre Company); Island (Belvoir
Street Theatre); Romeo & Juliet, Richard III,
Hamlet (Bell Shakespeare Company).
Television includes: I Saw You, Tenth Kingdom.
Film includes: 3 Guesses, The Abduction Club,
Ritual, The Journeyman, Double Jeopardy,
Elephant Juice, Brokedown Palace, 54, Say You'll
Be Mine, 1999, Dangerous Beauty, Polish
Wedding, Muriel's Wedding.

Christopher Oram (designer)
Theatre includes: The Marriage Play/Finding the
Sun, Summerfolk (RNT); Don Juan, Edward II,
As You Like It, Six Degrees of Separation,
Twelfth Night, What the Butler Saw (Crucible,
Sheffield); Merrily We Roll Along, Passion Play,
Good, The Bullet (Donmar); Dinner With
Friends (Hampstead); The Jew of Malta, The
Doctor's Dilemma (Almeida); A Life (Abbey,
Dublin); Aristocrats (Gate, Dublin); A Streetcar
Named Desire, All My Sons (Bristol Old Vic).

Nina Raine (assistant director)
For the Royal Court: Mountain Language/Ashes
To Ashes, Presence, Mouth To Mouth, Far Away,
My Zinc Bed.
Theatre includes: Passion Play, Miss Julie (Burton
Taylor Theatre, Oxford); The Way of the World
(for the Red Cross at Trebinshwyn); Ashes to
Ashes, Old Vic New Voices (Old Vic).
Nina's work on this production is supported by
the Channel Four/Royal Court Theatre Drama
Directors Programme.

Johanna Town (lighting designer)
Johanna has been Head of Lighting for the
Royal Court since 1990 and has designed
extensively for the company during this time.
Productions include: Nightingale and Chase,
Sliding With Suzanne (co-production with Out of
Joint), I Just Stopped By To See The Man, Under
the Blue Sky, Mr Kolpert, Other People, Toast,
The Kitchen, Faith Healer, Pale Horse, Search
and Destroy.
Other recent theatre designs include: Top Girls
(OSC); Les Liaison Dangereuses (Liverpool
Playhouse); Feelgood (Out of Joint/ Hampstead/
Garrick); Playboy of the Western World
(Liverpool Playhouse); Rita, Sue and Bob Too, A
State Affair (Out of Joint/Soho Theatre); Arabian
Nights (New Victory, New York); Ghosts (Royal
Exchange Theatre); Our Lady of Sligo (Irish
Repertory Theatre, New York); Rose (RNT/
Broadway); Little Malcolm (Hampstead/ West
End); Our Country's Good (Young Vic/Out of
Joint); Blue Heart (Royal Court/Out of Joint/
New York); Tobias and the Angel (Almeida
Opera Festival).

AWARDS FOR
THE ROYAL COURT

Terry Johnson's Hysteria won the 1994 Olivier Award for Best Comedy, and also the Writers' Guild Award for Best West End Play. Kevin Elyot's My Night with Reg won the 1994 Writers' Guild Award for Best Fringe Play, the Evening Standard Award for Best Comedy, and the 1994 Olivier Award for Best Comedy. Joe Penhall was joint winner of the 1994 John Whiting Award for Some Voices. Sebastian Barry won the 1995 Writers' Guild Award for Best Fringe Play, the 1995 Critics' Circle Award and the 1997 Christopher Ewart-Biggs Literary Prize for The Steward of Christendom, and the 1995 Lloyds Private Banking Playwright of the Year Award. Jez Butterworth won the 1995 George Devine Award for Most Promising Playwright, the 1995 Writers' Guild New Writer of the Year Award, the Evening Standard Award for Most Promising Playwright and the 1995 Olivier Award for Best Comedy for Mojo.

The Royal Court was the overall winner of the 1995 Prudential Award for the Arts for creativity, excellence, innovation and accessibility. The Royal Court Theatre Upstairs won the 1995 Peter Brook Empty Space Award for innovation and excellence in theatre.

Michael Wynne won the 1996 Meyer-Whitworth Award for The Knocky. Martin McDonagh won the 1996 George Devine Award, the 1996 Writers' Guild Best Fringe Play Award, the 1996 Critics' Circle Award and the 1996 Evening Standard Award for Most Promising Playwright for The Beauty Queen of Leenane. Marina Carr won the 19th Susan Smith Blackburn Prize (1996/7) for Portia Coughlan. Conor McPherson won the 1997 George Devine Award, the 1997 Critics' Circle Award and the 1997 Evening Standard Award for Most Promising Playwright for The Weir. Ayub Khan-Din won the 1997 Writers' Guild Awards for Best West End Play and Writers' Guild New Writer of the Year and the 1996 John Whiting Award for East is East. Anthony Neilson won the 1997 Writers' Guild Award for Best Fringe Play for The Censor.

At the 1998 Tony Awards, Martin McDonagh's The Beauty Queen of Leenane (co-production with Druid Theatre Company) won four awards including Garry Hynes for Best Director and was nominated for a further two. Eugene Ionesco's The Chairs (co-production with Theatre de Complicite) was nominated for six Tony awards. David Hare won the 1998 Time Out Live Award for Outstanding Achievement and six awards in New York including the Drama League, Drama Desk and New York Critics Circle Award for Via Dolorosa. Sarah Kane won the 1998 Arts Foundation Fellowship in Playwriting. Rebecca

Prichard won the 1998 Critics' Circle Award for Most Promising Playwright for Yard Gal (co-production with Clean Break).

Conor McPherson won the 1999 Olivier Award for Best New Play for The Weir. The Royal Court won the 1999 ITI Award for Excellence in International Theatre. Sarah Kane's Cleansed was judged Best Foreign Language Play in 1999 by Theater Heute in Germany. Gary Mitchell won the 1999 Pearson Best Play Award for Trust. Rebecca Gilman was joint winner of the 1999 George Devine Award and won the 1999 Evening Standard Award for Most Promising Playwright for The Glory of Living.

Roy Williams and Gary Mitchell were joint winners of the George Devine Award 2000 for Most Promising Playwright for Lift Off and The Force of Change respectively. At the Barclays Theatre Awards 2000 presented by the TMA, Richard Wilson won the Best Director Award for David Gieselmann's Mr Kolpert and Jeremy Herbert won the Best Designer Award for Sarah Kane's 4.48 Psychosis. Gary Mitchell won the Evening Standard's Charles Wintour Award 2000 for Most Promising Playwright for The Force of Change. Stephen Jeffreys' I Just Stopped by to See The Man won an AT&T: On Stage Award 2000. David Eldridge's Under the Blue Sky won the Time Out Live Award 2001 for Best New Play in the West End. Leo Butler won the George Devine Award 2001 for Most Promising Playwright for Redundant.

In 1999, the Royal Court won the European theatre prize New Theatrical Realities, presented at Taormina Arte in Sicily, for its efforts in recent years in discovering and producing the work of young British dramatists.

ROYAL COURT BOOKSHOP

The bookshop offers a wide range of playtexts and the best in theatre writing of the 20th and 21st Century. Located in the downstairs Bar and Food, the bookshop is open Monday to Saturday, afternoons and evenings.

Many Royal Court playtexts are available for just £2 including works by Harold Pinter, Caryl Churchill, Rebecca Gilman, Martin Crimp, Sarah Kane, Conor McPherson, Marina Carr, Ayub Khan-Din, Timberlake Wertenbaker and Roy Williams.

For information on titles and special events, Email: bookshop@royalcourttheatre.com
Tel: 020 7565 5024

THE ENGLISH STAGE COMPANY
AT THE ROYAL COURT

The English Stage Company at the Royal Court opened in 1956 as a subsidised theatre producing new British plays, international plays and some classical revivals.

The first artistic director George Devine aimed to create a writers' theatre, 'a place where the dramatist is acknowledged as the fundamental creative force in the theatre and where the play is more important than the actors, the director, the designer'. The urgent need was to find a contemporary style in which the play, the acting, direction and design are all combined. He believed that 'the battle will be a long one to continue to create the right conditions for writers to work in'.

Devine aimed to discover 'hard-hitting, uncompromising writers whose plays are stimulating, provocative and exciting'. The Royal Court production of John Osborne's Look Back in Anger in May 1956 is now seen as the decisive starting point of modern British drama and the policy created a new generation of British playwrights. The first wave included John Osborne, Arnold Wesker, John Arden, Ann Jellicoe, N F Simpson and Edward Bond. Early seasons included new international plays by Bertolt Brecht, Eugène Ionesco, Samuel Beckett, Jean-Paul Sartre and Marguerite Duras.

The theatre started with the 400-seat proscenium arch Theatre Downstairs, and then in 1969 opened a second theatre, the 60-seat studio Theatre Upstairs. Some productions transfer to the West End, such as Caryl Churchill's Far Away, Conor McPherson's The Weir, Kevin Elyot's Mouth to Mouth and My Night With Reg. The Royal Court also co-produces plays which have transferred to the West End or toured internationally, such as Sebastian Barry's The Steward of Christendom and Mark Ravenhill's Shopping and Fucking (with Out of Joint), Martin McDonagh's The Beauty Queen Of Leenane (with Druid Theatre Company), Ayub Khan-Din's East is East (with Tamasha Theatre Company, and now a feature film).

Since 1994 the Royal Court's artistic policy has again been vigorously directed to finding and producing a new generation of playwrights. The writers include Joe Penhall, Rebecca Prichard, Michael Wynne, Nick Grosso, Judy Upton, Meredith Oakes, Sarah Kane, Anthony Neilson, Judith Johnson, James Stock, Jez Butterworth, Marina Carr, Simon Block, Martin McDonagh, Mark Ravenhill, Ayub Khan-Din, Tamantha Hammerschlag, Jess Walters, Che Walker, Conor McPherson, Simon Stephens, Richard Bean, Roy

photo: Andy Chopping

Williams, Gary Mitchell, Mick Mahoney, Rebecca Gilman, Christopher Shinn, Kia Corthron, David Gieselmann, Marius von Mayenburg, David Eldridge, Leo Butler, Zinnie Harris and Grae Cleugh. This expanded programme of new plays has been made possible through the support of A.S.K Theater Projects, the Jerwood Charitable Foundation, the American Friends of the Royal Court Theatre and many in association with the Royal National Theatre Studio.

In recent years there have been record-breaking productions at the box office, with capacity houses for Jez Butterworth's Mojo, Sebastian Barry's The Steward of Christendom, Martin McDonagh's The Beauty Queen of Leenane, Ayub Khan-Din's East is East, Eugène Ionesco's The Chairs, David Hare's My Zinc Bed and Conor McPherson's The Weir, which transferred to the West End in October 1998 and ran for nearly two years at the Duke of York's Theatre.

The newly refurbished theatre in Sloane Square opened in February 2000, with a policy still inspired by the first artistic director George Devine. The Royal Court is an international theatre for new plays and new playwrights, and the work shapes contemporary drama in Britain and overseas.

REBUILDING THE ROYAL COURT

In 1995, the Royal Court was awarded a National Lottery grant through the Arts Council of England, to pay for three quarters of a £26m project to completely rebuild its 100-year old home. The rules of the award required the Royal Court to raise £7.6m in partnership funding. The building has been completed thanks to the generous support of those listed below.

We are particularly grateful for the contributions of over 5,700 audience members.

English Stage Company Registered Charity number 231242.

THE AMERICAN FRIENDS OF THE ROYAL COURT THEATRE

AFRCT support the mission of the Royal Court and are primarily focused on raising funds to enable the theatre to produce new work by emerging American writers. Since this not-for-profit organisation was founded in 1997, AFRCT has contributed to seven productions including Rebecca Gilman's Boy Gets Girl. They have also supported the participation of young artists in the Royal Court's acclaimed International Residency.

If you would like to support the ongoing work of the Royal Court, please contact the Development Department on 020 7565 5050.

PROGRAMME SUPPORTERS

The Royal Court (English Stage Company Ltd) receives its principal funding from London Arts. It is also supported financially by a wide range of private companies and public bodies and earns the remainder of its income from the box office and its own trading activities.

The Royal Borough of Kensington & Chelsea gives an annual grant to the Royal Court Young Writers' Programme and the London Boroughs Grants Committee provides project funding for a number of play development initiatives.

The Jerwood Charitable Foundation continues to support new plays by new playwrights through the Jerwood New Playwrights series. Since 1993 the A.S.K. Theater Projects of Los Angeles has funded a Playwrights' Programme at the theatre. Bloomberg Mondays, the Royal Court's reduced price ticket scheme, is supported by Bloomberg.

TRUSTS AND FOUNDATIONS
American Friends of the Royal Court Theatre
Anon
The Carnegie United Kingdom Trust
Carlton Television Trust
Gerald Chapman Fund
Cultural Foundation Deutsche Bank
The Foundation for Sport and the Arts
The Genesis Foundation
The Goldsmiths' Company
Jerwood Charitable Foundation
John Lyon's Charity
The Laura Pels Foundation
Quercus Charitable Trust
The Peggy Ramsay Foundation
The Peter Jay Sharp Foundation
The Royal Victoria Hall Foundation
The Sobell Foundation
The Trusthouse Charitable Foundation
Garfield Weston Foundation

MAJOR SPONSORS
Amerada Hess
A.S.K. Theater Projects
AT&T: OnStage
Barclays plc
BBC
Bloomberg
Channel Four
Royal College of Psychiatrists

BUSINESS MEMBERS
BP
CGNU plc
J Walter Thompson
Lazard
Lever Fabergé
McCABES
Pemberton Greenish
Peter Jones
Redwood
SIEMENS
Simons Muirhead & Burton

INDIVIDUAL MEMBERS
Patrons
Anon

David H Adams
Advanpress
Katie Bradford
Mrs Alan Campbell-Johnson
Gill Carrick
David Coppard
Chris Corbin
David Day
Thomas Fenton
Ralph A Fields
John Flower
Mike Frain
Edna & Peter Goldstein
David R & Catherine Graham
Homevale Ltd
Tamara Ingram
Mr & Mrs Jack Keenan
JHJ & SF Lewis
Lex Service plc
Barbara Minto
Michael & Mimi Naughton
New Penny Productions Ltd
Martin Newson
AT Poeton & Son Ltd.
André Ptaszynski, Really
William & Hilary Russell
Useful Theatres
Carolin Quentin
Ian & Carol Sellars
Bernard Shapero
Miriam Stoppard
Carl & Martha Tack
Jan & Michael Topham
Mr & Mrs Anthony Weldon
Richard Wilson OBE

Benefactors
Anon
Anastasia Alexander
Lesley E Alexander
Judith Asalache
Batia Asher
Elaine Mitchell Attias
Thomas Bendhem
Mark Bentley
Jody Berger
Keith & Helen Bolderson
Jeremy Bond
Eleanor Bowden
Brian Boylan
Mr & Mrs F H Bradley III
Mrs Elly Brook JP
Julian Brookstone
Paul & Ossi Burger
Debbi & Richard Burston
Yuen-Wei Chew

Martin Cliff
Carole & Neville Conrad
Conway Van Gelder
Coppard & Co.
Barry Cox
Curtis Brown Ltd
Deborah Davis
Chris & Jane Deering
Zöe Dominic
Robyn Durie
Lorraine Esdaile
Winston & Jean Fletcher
Claire & William Frankel
Nick Fraser
J Garcia
Beverley & Nathaniel Gee
Norman Gerard
Jacqueline & Jonathan Gestetner
Michael Goddard
Carolyn Goldbart
Judy & Frank Grace
Sally Greene
Byron Grote
Sue & Don Guiney
Hamilton Asper Management
Woodley Hapgood
Jan Harris
Phil Hobbs
Anna Home OBE
Amanda Howard Associates
Mrs Martha Hummer-Bradley
Trevor Ingman
Lisa Irwin-Burgess
Peter Jones
Paul Kaju & Jane Peterson
Peter & Maria Kellner
Diana King
Clico Kingsbury
Lee & Thompson
Caroline & Robert Lee
Carole A Leng
Lady Lever
Colette & Peter Levy
Ann Lewis
Ian Mankin
Christopher Marcus
David Marks
Alan & Tricia Marshall
Nicola McFarland
James McIvor
Mr & Mrs Roderick R McManigal
Mae Modiano

Eva Monley
Pat Morton
Georgia Oetker
Paul Oppenheimer
Janet & Michael Orr
Diana Parker
Maria Peacock
Pauline Pinder
JTG Philipson QC
Jeremy Priestley
John & Rosemarie Reynolds
Samuel French Ltd
Bernice & Victor Sandelson
John Sandoe (Books) Ltd
Nicholas Selmes
Jenny Sheridan
Lois Sieff OBE
Peregrine Simon
Brian D Smith
John Soderquist
Max Stafford-Clark
Sue Stapely
Ann Marie Starr
June Summerill
Anthony Wigram
George & Moira Yip
Georgia Zaris

STAGE HANDS CIRCLE
Graham Billing
Andrew Cryer
Lindy Fletcher
Susan Hayden
Mr R Hopkins
Philip Hughes Trust
Dr A V Jones
Roger Jospe
Miss A Lind-Smith
Mr J Mills
Nevin Charitable Trust
Janet & Michael Orr
Jeremy Priestley
Ann Scurfield
Brian Smith
Harry Streets
Richard Wilson OBE
C C Wright

FOR THE ROYAL COURT

JERWOOD
NEW PLAYWRIGHTS

Since 1993 Jerwood New Playwrights have contributed to some of the Royal Court's most successful productions, including SHOPPING AND FUCKING by Mark Ravenhill (co-production with Out of Joint), EAST IS EAST by Ayub Khan-Din (co-production with Tamasha), THE BEAUTY QUEEN OF LEENANE by Martin McDonagh (co-production with Druid Theatre Company), THE WEIR by Conor McPherson, REAL CLASSY AFFAIR by Nick Grosso, THE FORCE OF CHANGE by Gary Mitchell, ON RAFTERY'S HILL by Marina Carr (co-production with Druid Theatre Company), 4.48 PSYCHOSIS by Sarah Kane, UNDER THE BLUE SKY by David Eldridge, PRESENCE by David Harrower, HERONS by Simon Stephens and CLUBLAND by Roy Williams.

The Jerwood Charitable Foundation is a registered charity dedicated to imaginative and responsible funding and sponsorship of the arts, education, design and other areas of human endeavour and excellence. This season Jerwood New Playwrights are supporting REDUNDANT by Leo Butler, NIGHTINGALE AND CHASE by Zinnie Harris and FUCKING GAMES by Grae Cleugh.

HERONS by Simon Stephens
(photo: Pete Jones)

EAST IS EAST by Ayub Khan-Din
(photo: Robert Day)

Fucking Games

*for my mother Marion Cleugh
and my best friend Garrick Jones*

Characters

Terrence, aged forty-nine.
Jonah, aged thirty-five.
Jude, aged twenty-nine.
Danny, aged twenty.

Terrence, **Jonah** and **Jude** are from London. **Danny** is from Glasgow.

Setting

The play is set in the living room of **Terrence** and **Jonah**'s house in Chelsea, London. The action takes place in the present, on a summer evening.

Note

An oblique/stroke used in dialogue is the cue for the next speaker to interrupt the first.

Acknowledgements

I would like to thank Dominic Cooke, Graham Whybrow, Nick Marston, Ian Rickson, Lisa Makin, Diane Borger and Ewan Thomson for their tremendous support, encouragement, wise advice and patience and for their faith in this play; the entire team at the Royal Court for being such professionals and such a joy to work with and finally Hugh Hodgart, Head of Acting at the Royal Scottish Academy of Music and Drama, for his encouragement, support and for giving me the space to make this happen.

Act One

Scene One

There is one door, stage left, which leads into the hall. The overall look of the room is chic and minimalist. Centre stage are two long matching sofas in a wide V shape and facing the audience, and a coffee table in the middle on which sits a cigarette box, a large cigarette lighter, an ashtray and a few magazines. Behind there are two windows, one left, one right. Between the two windows is a large modern art painting, a 'Damien Hirst' or similar. Downstage left is a television/video system, and downstage right is a CD/music system. Stage-right middle there is a cabinet, on which a telephone sits. Across from this, stage-left middle, is another matching cabinet which functions as a drinks/drugs cabinet. The whole effect is to create a symmetrical-looking room, each half being almost a mirror image of the other.

On the rise, **Jonah** *is sitting on the sofa stage left, with* **Terrence** *restlessly sitting on the other sofa. They are having drinks and smoking cigarettes – all four characters smoke at their discretion throughout. Nothing is said for some moments. Then* **Terrence** *gets up and removes a box from the cabinet stage left. He brings it over to the coffee table and sits back down. He takes out a mirror and some other drugs paraphernalia from the box, and starts cutting cocaine.*

Terrence   Do you want?

There is no answer from **Jonah**. **Terrence** *carries on.*

Jonah   Can't you wait?

Terrence *does a line, puts the cocaine and paraphernalia back in the box and replaces it.*

Terrence   What's the issue?

Jonah   Every time there's a new one we have to have a drinks party.

Terrence   He's just seeking approval.

Jonah   From you?

Terrence   Yes.

Jonah   Please.

Terrence   These chickens he brings around. I call it as I see it.

Jonah   Yes.

Terrence   Anyway, he said that this one tonight is different, special.

Jonah   He always says they're special.

Terrence   Yes he does, doesn't he? Another drink, my darling?

Jonah *looks at him with disapproval.*

Terrence   What else is there to do?

Jonah *shows his glass to* **Terrence**. *He collects it and moves to the drinks cabinet.*

Jonah   You could always take a turn in the park. It is dark now.

Terrence   I'm not that desperate.

Jonah   You were on Friday.

Terrence   I beg your pardon?

Jonah   Last Friday night, when I was away. You *bumped into* Tim there. I was speaking to him this morning.

Terrence   Yes that's right. I forgot.

Jonah   Did you meet anyone?

Terrence   I did actually.

Jonah   Did he have a name?

Terrence   I'm sure he did.

Jonah   Cute or pot ugly?

Terrence *returns with the drinks and sits down.*

Terrence   You know I only ever go for the cute ones.

Jonah   And?

Terrence   I was up for a fuck but he wasn't, so I let him suck me off. He was good.

He lights a cigarette and inhales deeply.

Did you get up to anything in Brighton over the weekend?

Jonah   I met someone.

Terrence   Where?

Jonah   I went to a brothel.

Terrence   I didn't know they had brothels in Brighton.

Jonah   They have one.

Terrence   Really?

Jonah   That's right.

Terrence   Mm.

Jonah   What?

Terrence   What was he like then?

Jonah   Cheap, and very young.

Terrence   How young?

Jonah   He said he was eighteen. I think it was nearer sixteen.

Terrence   And what was his name, this child?

Jonah   Does it matter?

Terrence   And you fucked him of course.

Jonah   That's right.

He offers **Jonah** *a cigarette.* **Jonah** *refuses. Beat.*

Jonah   What?

No response. A long pause. The doorbell goes. Without hesitation,
Jonah *exits. Offstage left we hear the front door opening and the*
following voices:

Jonah   Hi! Please come in.

Jude   This is Danny. Danny, this is Jonah.

Jonah   How do you do?

Danny   Amazing house.

Jonah   Go straight through.

Jude *and* **Danny** *enter, followed by* Jonah.

Jude   Hi. How are you?

Terrence *and* **Jude** *awkwardly double kiss on the cheeks, fashion-style.*

Terrence   Fine. You look nice.

Jude   Thanks. This is Danny.

Terrence   Hi.

Danny   I've heard a lot about you.

Beat.

Jonah   Please sit down. Would you like a drink?

Jonah *moves to the drinks cabinet.* **Jude** *points* **Danny** *to the sofa stage right and they make their way to it.* **Terrence** *sits on the sofa stage left.*

Jude   I'll have my usual. Danny?

Danny   Just a Coke for me please.

Terrence   Don't you drink? Or perhaps you're under age?

Danny   No, not for anything.

Terrence   Really?

Danny   I'm twenty.

Terrence   You look younger.

Danny   So they tell me.

Terrence   Do you like vodka?

Danny   Sure.

Terrence   Jonah, put a vodka in that Coke.

Jonah   If he just wants a Coke, let him have a Coke.

Terrence   Go on, Danny, have a proper drink. It'll help loosen things up.

Danny   A Coke will be fine.

Terrence   I don't want you to feel left out.

Danny   That's okay. I don't mind.

Jonah *finishes making the drinks.*

Jonah   Okay!

He brings drinks over for **Jude** *and* **Danny**.

There we are.

Jude   Thank you.

Danny   Thanks.

Jonah *then brings drinks over for himself and* **Terrence**, *and sits beside him.*

Jonah   How are things?

Jude   Great. I'm about to do a commercial for a new collection of skin-care products for men.

Jonah   A job? My God!

Jude   It's quite interesting actually. There's a special new ingredient they're using that no other product on the market has.

Terrence   What is it?

Jude   They're not telling, not until I do the job.

Terrence   Very hush-hush. What are the products called?

Jude   They're called the 'Mr X' range.

Jonah   Sounds a bit tacky, don't you think?

Terrence   Secrecy and anonymity – I'm interested. So, what will these products do that others can't? Why would I want to buy this latest pink-pound ploy?

Jude   The idea is that they preserve the skin for longer by adding a special layer of moisturising protection on top of it. It will give you a second face on top of the one you already have.

Jonah   I doubt if Terrence would have need of that.

Terrence   That's right, darling. I'm a great believer in 'what you see is what you get'.

Beat.

Jude   And you?

Jonah   What?

Jude   How is work with you?

Jonah   The same.

Danny   What do you do?

Jonah   I run a private members club.

Danny   What like?

Terrence   It's called 'R & R'. Like the Groucho – only better. Do you know it?

Danny   Course I do. Just opened, Soho, Bateman Street.

Terrence   You've been in?

Danny   Not yet. I've heard good things about it.

Terrence   That's nice to hear – because I own it.

Danny   Wow.

Terrence   Yes.

Danny   Jonah and you are partners?

Terrence   Only in one sense. Jonah works for me, don't you, darling?

There is no reply from **Jonah**.

I own it and Jonah runs it for me.

Danny   You landed on your feet there, eh?

Jonah   Oh yes.

Terrence   Oh no. Jonah worked his way up the *hard* way, didn't you? Jonah was a waiter in my first restaurant and I really quite fancied him – that was ten years ago – we started going out, and he worked so *hard* he quickly worked his way up to become my *Head* Waiter. He was such a good *Head* Waiter that I made him my *Head* Manager. He's done well out of it ever since, haven't you, runs the smartest place in London, meets the happening people, above all else he's made sure the money has kept rolling in, and the thing about money – the really important thing about money – money can make you a very popular guy. Sometimes I think that my money is one of the few attractive qualities I have left. (*To* **Jonah**.) What do you think darling? (*No response.*) And you two, what do you think?

Beat.

Danny   I'm sure that can't be true.

Terrence   Tell me, what do you do? Hairdresser, nurse, fashion student or airline steward?

Jude   Danny's a DJ. He has his own night every Thursday downstairs at the 333 club in Hoxton. It's called 'Subversion'.

Terrence   Another gay club, I suppose.

Danny   Actually it's mixed.

Terrence   Mixed? Does that really work? I've never understood the point of having a gay club if you let straight people in.

Danny   The whole gay ghetto thing is dying on its arse. Nobody cares any more. My club is about the music.

Terrence   What kind of music is that?

Danny   Speed garage.

Terrence   What's that?

Jonah   That's like Kwik-Fit. You know, those boys in the blue boiler suits that you like.

Terrence   That was funny, Jonah.

Jonah   Surely you've heard of speed garage Terrence?

Terrence   No.

Jonah   Showing your age a bit, aren't you?

Terrence   Belt up, bitch.

Jonah   Do you know what age Terrence is going to be this year, Danny?

Terrence   Shut up. Let's not bore Danny with that.

Jonah   Go on, Danny. Don't be shy. Take a guess.

Danny   I have no idea.

Jonah   Come on. You can take a guess at least. Terrence won't be offended if you get it wrong, will you, Terrence?

Terrence   Don't push me, Jonah.

Jonah   What do you say, Danny, have a guess. Come on now, have a guess!

Danny   Thirty-eight?

Jonah   Danny, I've heard of erring on the side of caution but that's ridiculous.

Terrence   That's enough, Jonah. I mean it.

Jonah   Come on, Danny. There's no need to be polite. Take a real guess. People always appreciate honesty more in my experience. Go on. Go on now!

Terrence *is about to interrupt again.*

Danny   Fifty?

Jonah   Fifty! Yes! The grand old age of fifty. The big five-oh. There'll be a huge party at the club if I get my way, it's not the sort of thing you can let go by without a fanfare, is it? And there'll be a massive cake, I thought that instead of candles, we could use fifty dildos. It would make for quite a statement – fifty burning cocks. Like a big, gay bonfire night.

Terrence   If there's going to be a bonfire, you really must be 'the guy', Jonah?

Jonah   No. Not me. I'll never be 'the guy', Terrence – will I?

Terrence (*to* **Danny**)   Fifty. What do you think of that?

Danny   Personally, I've always thought this obsession about age was bullshit.

Terrence   That's easy to say when you're what, twelve?

Danny   Twenty.

Terrence   Whatever.

Danny   I've gone out with older men.

Terrence   If you mean Jude, sweetie, he's still only twenty-nine. I have news for you – that's not old.

Danny   No, I went out with a guy your age.

Terrence   You're just full of surprises, aren't you, Danny?

Jude   I didn't know that.

Danny   It didn't last long.

Terrence   A bit too old for you after all?

Danny   Nothing so predictable.

Terrence   Well – I may need to watch myself around this one, boys.

Danny   You're safe enough.

Jonah *laughs*.

Terrence   You do look very good tonight, Jude. Did I say that already?

Jude   A girl can never hear that too much.

Terrence   In our world it's very important to look good. Without it you're nothing.

Jonah   Please.

Terrence   Danny? Don't you think Jude looks very good tonight?

Danny   Of course.

Terrence   You don't have to if you don't want to, Danny. It's not compulsory to say so because he's sitting there.

Danny   I wouldn't say it if I didn't think it.

Terrence   We must always say what we mean. It really is refreshing to have a good-looking man in the house.

Jude   Please Terrence, I'm embarrassed.

Terrence   Don't be. Credit where credit's due, Jude, and I'm very happy to give you the credit you deserve.

Jude   I appreciate it.

Terrence   Good. You're beautiful. I appreciate that. It's the kind of appreciation that comes with maturity. Kids don't have it, eh, Danny?

Danny   I never thought about it.

Terrence   You should. Jude is very beautiful, easy to find of course but harder to keep. Those eyes, those soft lips, that beautiful skin, that body. It pays to look after yourself.

Jude   Thank you, Terrence.

Terrence   You're very welcome.

Jonah *gets up to make the drinks.*

Jonah   I've never really gone for the 'beautiful' type myself.

Terrence   Really.

Jonah (*to* **Danny**)   Obviously. I've always preferred men who have an individual look, a little less perfect, a little more interesting.

Danny   I know what you mean. You get so fucking bored seeing all those old clones all looking the same all the time.

Jonah   One seems to be permanently faced with a choice between Greek gods who can barely string a sentence together, or at the opposite end of the market, seedy old queens who prey on young men, which is disgusting, most of them pay for it, I expect. What do you think, Jude?

Jude   I don't have an opinion.

Jonah   It's depressing, isn't it, Danny?

Danny   You said it.

Jonah   I don't see you in either one of those categories.

Danny   Don't think so.

Jonah   No. It's refreshing to come across someone like you.

Terrence   It would be if you could.

Jonah   One of Terrence's vile little interjections. He has quite a range. But, Danny, I mean it. You're different, special.

Danny   Thank you.

Jonah   *You're* very welcome.

Terrence *laughs.*

Jonah   What?

Terrence   Don't.

Jonah   Don't what, Terrence? Spit it out please, everyone knows you've had plenty of practice at that over the years.

Beat.

Terrence   Well Danny?

Danny   What?

Terrence   Tell me, would someone like you be interested in someone like Jonah?

Danny   I have no idea.

Terrence   It's just a hypothetical question.

Danny   I don't know.

Terrence   Come on. Would a funky kid like you be interested in this fagbutt of a man?

Jonah   That's enough.

Terrence   Is it? (*To* **Danny**.) Well?

Danny   I don't think I should get involved.

Terrence   Too late – Jonah's already done that.

Jonah   I haven't.

Terrence   You know you have.

Jonah   It's all right, Danny. Forget it. One of her moods. She's due to come on any time now.

Terrence   Yes, but not to you. Well, Danny, answer the question.

Danny   What question?

Terrence   Do you fancy Jonah?

Danny *turns to* **Jude** *for help.*

Terrence   Don't bother asking Jude. We can safely take his answer for granted.

Danny   I only came round for a drink.

Terrence   I know. You've had one. Now indulge us.

Jonah   Terrence!

Terrence   I'm asking the questions now, lover! Well!?

Danny   I don't know.

Terrence   You don't know!? Come on, Danny, it's not as difficult as all that is it? Or am I mistaken, you do fancy him, why don't you take him upstairs right now and fuck him!?

Danny   Terrence

Terrence   Well, do you fancy him or not!?

Danny   No.

Terrence   No!? No, of course not.

Jonah *finishes making the drinks, which he then brings over, all in silence. Beat.*

Danny (*to* **Jonah**)   Ten years? (*No response, again to* **Jonah**.) Ten years?

Terrence   Jonah. Danny's talking to you.

Jonah   I'm sorry. What did you say?

Danny   You've been together ten years?

Jonah   Almost.

Danny   When's your anniversary?

Jonah *doesn't answer, so* **Terrence** *does.*

Terrence   August. The . . .

Jonah   September the second. We met in August, our first date was September the second.

Terrence   I remember.

Jonah *looks at him.*

Terrence   Our first date – we went for dinner, to a Spanish restaurant in Soho, had a beautiful meal and went back to yours.

Jonah   The restaurant was called Encontro. It was Portuguese and in Notting Hill. It was Terrence's favourite restaurant at the time. Our waiter turned out to be someone you'd had a fling with, he was flirting with you the whole evening, was very amusing. His name was Nuno, he was cute. Later we went to Ronnie Scott's. We had a table in a corner, with a little lamp in the middle and we drank wine and listened to the jazz. We did go back to mine and I don't know why but I made milkshakes and we took them to bed. They were strawberry.

Terrence   Strawberry milkshakes. I remember.

Terrence *and* **Jonah** *have a moment together.*

Jude (*breaking the moment*)   Ten years. That's quite an achievement. Especially for a gay couple. Most gay men in relationships that long would need a change.

Jonah   A change?

Jude   For most couples it's going to get stale. You get bored with each other, stop having sex, don't go out any more, don't have any fun – you'd be bound to start looking elsewhere sooner or later, and who could blame you?

Danny   Is that really what you think?

Jude   I know from personal experience how hard it is for couples to make it work that long.

Danny   You haven't been in a long-term relationship.

Jude   I know. My parents got divorced last year. They're both much happier. It was traumatic at the time. Better that than staying in something that isn't working. Sometimes you have to be brave.

Danny   It's easy to walk when it's not working, it takes guts to stick with it. Of course things change after you've been together that long. If your relationship hasn't developed into something other than fucking and going to clubs, that's when you should be worried.

Terrence   The kid speaks out.

Jude   There comes a point when you must recognise that something is over.

Jonah   When?

Jude   When you just know. Then, get out.

Terrence   What do you think, Danny?

Danny   People shouldn't stay in loveless relationships. There are too many guys out there who've settled for less than they want because they're too fucking scared of being on their own. I've also met plenty of gay blokes who don't have the staying power to hold down a relationship for ten minutes.

Terrence   What are you looking for?

Danny   I want to meet someone, spend my life with him. I don't think that will happen. But, if I have to do this on my own, I will.

Terrence   What about Jude?

Danny   I like Jude.

Terrence   Why?

Danny   Why?

Terrence   What are his good qualities, apart from the obvious?

Jude   Don't talk about me like I'm not here please.

Danny   Jude has good stuff going on, if you scratch the surface you'll see it.

Jude   Thanks, Danny.

Terrence   Really?

Danny   Yes.

Terrence   Like what?

Danny   I'm sure you must know already, Terrence – don't you?

Beat.

Terrence   How did you two meet?

Jude   We met at Danny's club about a month ago.

Terrence   At a club, how original. And a whole month ago. That must be something of a record for Jude. We were thinking of having a revolving door fitted to his apartment, weren't we, Jonah? So, he must be special or something?

Jude   Yes.

Terrence   What's so special about you Danny?

Danny   I have a huge dick – does that count?

They laugh.

Terrence   Definitely. Tell me exactly how you met. I want to know all the details.

Danny   It's not that exciting.

Terrence   Try me.

Beat.

Danny I was DJing at the club, I had just finished my set, I was talking to Kate, who's my best friend / and . . .

Jude Kate is very beautiful.

Danny Yes. She likes you too.

Jude I'm glad.

There is a moment between **Jude** *and* **Danny**. **Terrence** *interrupts it.*

Terrence Beautiful. Not a dyke then.

Danny Definitely not a dyke. Anyway . . . Jude was looking over at me / and . . .

Terrence No, don't tell me. You sent your fag-hag girlfriend across to tell him, 'My mate fancies you.'

Danny No. He came over and started talking to me.

Terrence Jude came up to you?

Danny That's how we met.

Terrence That's a new one, you chatting someone up. Usually he just stands around and waits for the queue of eligible young bachelors to form.

Jude I almost didn't bother. I thought he was probably straight.

Terrence You do look a bit straight, Danny, we'll need to work on that, won't we Jonah?

Jonah I think he looks fine as he is.

Danny I've been thinking about that recently, I do want to change my look.

Terrence What did you have in mind?

Danny First of all I'm getting a number one – get rid of this awful hair. Then I was thinking about buying some nice, smart black trousers – or grey, they do say grey is the new black – Prada naturally, a couple of tight Helmut Lang tank tops to go with, a gorgeous pair of Patrick Cox's, join the gym of course, book some sunbeds, have my entire body waxed, and last but not least, chuck out all my garage records and get a whole new set of boy-band CDs. What do you think, girls? Do I get to join the club now?

Terrence   Maybe after your make-over. Right now, I'm not sure if the gay community's ready for you.

Danny   The gay community!? Yes, you're right. But then the idea of a community, as I understand it, is where people look out for each other. Most of what I've caught on the gay scene has been a bunch of narcissistic, tacky, cock-obsessed, sad fuck-ups who happen to share a common sexuality – I've never wanted to be part of that kind of community.

Terrence   You're just bursting with opinions, aren't you, Danny?

Danny   Probably just a young thing.

Beat.

Terrence   You were talking about you and Jude.

Danny   Jude came over, we started talking, I thought – I like this guy, I'm going to take him home.

Terrence   Simple as that?

Danny   Yes.

Terrence   I'm the same. If I see something I like, I go for it. I never let go of it once I've got it.

Danny   Like a dog with a bone.

Terrence   I bite as well as bark.

Danny   I'm thick-skinned.

Terrence   I like going in deep.

Beat.

Jude   Could I have another drink?

Jonah   I could use one too.

Jonah *gets up to make more drinks.*

Terrence   Do you like the place?

Danny   It's a lovely room.

Terrence   Would you like to see the rest of the house?

Danny   Sure.

Jude   Don't be too long with him, Terrence, will you?

Terrence   I thought Jonah might give Danny the tour.

Jonah   I'm making the drinks, Terrence.

Terrence   I'll take care of the drinks.

Jonah   Why don't you show Danny round, it was your idea.

Terrence   But the house is much more your department, Jonah, you'll be able to tell Danny what was done when. Go on.

Jonah   Danny?

Jonah *and* **Danny** *exit.* **Terrence** *gets up to finish making the drinks.*

Jude   You like him, don't you?

Terrence   He's a cocky little cunt.

Jude   But he is cute though, isn't he?

Terrence   Unlike you, Jude, I require more than a pretty face to impress me.

Jude   Since when?

Terrence   You're not seriously going to continue dating this boy?

Jude   I don't know yet.

Terrence   Come on.

Jude What?

Terrence He's all right for what he is . . .

Jude You're such a dreadful snob, Terrence.

Terrence He's not right for you.

Jude But you are?

Terrence I have Jonah.

Jude Who you're not in love with.

Terrence That's none of your business.

Jude It is my business. You promised me you would leave him.

Terrence You were probably sucking me off at the time.

Jude Did you tell him?

Terrence No.

Jude He knows anyway.

Terrence He doesn't know. He suspects. He'll never ask.

Jude Why not?

Terrence If he asks, he might get the answer he doesn't want.

Jude And us?

Terrence We go on as we are.

Beat.

Jude Perhaps I will give Danny and me a go – just me and him.

Terrence You can do so much better.

Jude Why don't you want me to have a boyfriend?

Terrence What?

Jude Why do you bad-mouth everyone I bring here?

Terrence   You only bring them here to make me jealous.

Jude   Not Danny.

Beat.

Terrence   Have you told him about us?

Jude   Sort of.

Terrence   What?

Jude   It came up that I've been having an affair . . . with someone who's already in a relationship . . . an older man.

Terrence   For God's sake. Do you know how much damage that big mouth of yours could do, you stupid boy?

Jude   Damage? To you.

Terrence   To me.

Jude   You're priceless, sweetie, you really are. He wants me to give you up.

Terrence   What?

Jude   He wants me to finish it and have a relationship with him.

Terrence   You in a monogamous relationship?

Jude   I told him I'd think about it.

Beat.

I want to see how much I mean to you.

Terrence   You should know by now how much you mean to me. What do you have in mind? Do you want me to fight him for you? Handbags at dawn? I can destroy that little cunt in a sentence.

Jude   He's smarter than you think.

Terrence   Then I'm surprised he hasn't seen through you yet. He seems to despise everything you represent.

Jude   A lot has happened over this last month that we've been together.

Terrence   What do you mean?

Jude   A lot's been shared between us.

Terrence   Do you mean cum? Or something important?

Jude   It's private.

Terrence   There's nothing private between us.

Jude   I won't.

Terrence   Tell me.

Beat.

Jude   I told him I'm in love with him.

Terrence   What?

Jude   Yes.

Beat.

Terrence   And?

Jude   And what?

Terrence   What are you going to do about it?

Beat.

Jude   I haven't decided.

Beat.

Terrence   You little bastard. Come here.

Jude   What?

Terrence   Come over here.

Jude   What for?

Terrence   I want you to go down on me right now.

Jude   They're upstairs.

Terrence   Be quick then.

Jude   I won't.

Terrence   You will.

Jude *moves to the other sofa and* **Terrence** *starts kissing him passionately.* **Jude**, *back to the audience, performs oral sex on* **Terrence**. *They try to keep the noise down and it is all over quickly.*

Terrence   In love with him.

Blackout.

Scene Two

Terrence *is sitting exactly as he was at the end of Scene One. There is someone at his feet as* **Jude** *was at the end of Scene One. After a moment,* **Danny** *comes up with a contact lens on the tip of his finger.*

Danny   Got it.

Terrence   So you have.

Danny *passes him the lens, thinks about sitting down next to him, and then crosses to the other sofa and sits down.* **Terrence** *watches him do this and then puts in his contact lens.*

Terrence   You wouldn't believe how many I've had and lost over the years.

Danny   Yes I would. I wear them too.

Beat.

Terrence   I like you, Danny.

Danny   Are you sure?

Terrence   Yes. I'm curious about you. Tell me about yourself. Drink?

Danny   Sure.

Terrence *gets up to make the drinks.*

Danny   I'm a lot like you, I think.

Terrence   How?

Danny   What you see is what you get.

Beat.

Terrence   Are your parents still in Scotland?

Danny   They're dead.

Terrence   I'm sorry.

Danny   They're not really dead. I say they are because I hate them and they hate me.

Terrence   Did they reject you after you came out?

Danny   Yes, of the womb. It's not a gay thing. They're just not my kind of people.

Terrence   Any brothers and sisters?

Danny   Just me.

Terrence   And how long have you been out?

Danny   Long enough. About nine months.

Terrence   Nine months?

Danny   Yes.

Terrence   Anything special so far?

Danny   Lots of one-night stands. I've seen more dicks this year than I would care to mention.

Terrence   Seen one, seen them all, eh? Sometimes it feels like I have seen them all.

Danny   Jude is the longest. Not dick. Relationship.

Terrence   You've only been seeing him for a month.

Danny   That's right.

Terrence   That's your longest relationship?

Danny Well . . . I . . .

Terrence It's nothing to be ashamed of Danny. I know how it is.

Danny I'm not ashamed. Because I'm not like that.

Terrence If you say so. It's hard to believe, you have so many strong views on relationships, for someone who has all the experience of a month to work from, it's just rather amusing. (*Starts laughing.*)

Danny Well /

Terrence Don't worry about it.

Danny It's /

Terrence It's not a problem

Danny I /

Terrence You're twenty. What else could I expect?

Danny Wait a fucking minute! Not that it's any of your business, but there was someone before Jude, I'm talking years not a month.

Terrence I meant something serious, not some high-school romance.

Danny I'm talking about someone I met when I was seventeen and went out with for over two years, who I was in love with and still love, and even lived with.

Terrence I stand corrected. I apologise. You should have said. But I don't understand.

Danny What?

Terrence You said you've only been out for nine months.

Danny So?

Terrence This relationship you're measuring in years – was it a boy?

Danny   I don't want to talk about it.

Beat.

Terrence   Was it your friend Kate?

Beat.

Let me offer you some advice, Danny. You're gay, you're twenty. You should be out there fucking everything that moves. You're still all loved up with Jude, so you should be after just a month. It won't last. It never does. Sooner or later you're going to get bored, and you're going to want someone else's hands on you and tongue in your mouth and dick inside you. It will happen. Jude will get hurt, as Jude always does, and then you'll lose a friend too. Why don't you just let him down gently now? Keep him as a friend, fuck him for a while if you want – it really is much easier this way. I know.

Danny   I've had plenty of fucks. I want something better.

Terrence   You're serious. Then you should know this. Jude is looking for someone who can look after him.

Danny   Maybe he should go on the game.

Terrence   There are subtler methods available. Most of the time Jude is an out-of-work actor, not because he needs to be but because he chooses to be. I've seen his work, he's good. But he can't be arsed. He likes an easy life.

Danny   So?

Terrence   You can't keep him.

Danny   Why?

Terrence   Because *you* can't *keep* him.

Danny   I can change him.

Terrence   No – you can't.

Danny   I'm going to try.

Terrence   Jude already has a lover. There are no vacancies.

Danny   He's going to give him up – for me.

Terrence   He won't.

Danny   Let's see

Terrence   His lover is well connected in London. He could help you with your club, with your music, get it moved to a better venue, introduce you to some industry people, help with some of your expenses perhaps. Why don't you think about it?

Danny   If he loves Jude that much why he doesn't do the honest thing and leave his boyfriend.

Terrence   At your tender age, I don't expect you to see the many shades of grey that there are in relationships, it's all a little more complex than you imagine.

Danny   I see them, those dirty shades of grey. My music and my club are going fine. I don't need any extra help.

Terrence   We all need extra, Danny. Why don't you just give him up.

Danny   Why don't you?

The front door is heard opening and closing. Enter **Jonah** *first, carrying some bags, then* **Jude**.

Jonah   I got the Stolly, Pernod and the Tanqueray. I got the champagne too. They had Moet but I thought Veuve would be nicer. I'll put the bubbles in the fridge and we can have those later.

Terrence   Later.

Jonah *puts the spirits on the drinks table and exits with the champagne.*

Jude   Sorry we were so long. There was a very cute guy in a very expensive Armani suit in front of us in the queue. I

got chatting to him. Italian. Gorgeous. Has a boat in
Chelsea Harbour. And a girlfriend. He thinks he's straight
but I had him sussed out in a minute. What have you two
been talking about?

Terrence   The generous rewards of monogamy.

Jonah *re-enters and moves to get the drinks.*

Terrence   I'll get them. Danny takes a very dim view of
people who are not completely faithful to each other. Not
having had a serious relationship before, with a man, he has
the luxury of being able to hold this opinion.

Danny   What's so unusual about monogamy? It's what
most people do.

Terrence   Wrong. It's what most straight people do.
We're not like the breeders. A lovely tasteful wedding in
peach, three screaming kids, a nice semi in Zone 5, a
Mondeo in the driveway, the shopping centre on Saturday,
the garden centre on Sunday, *Coronation Street* and *Who
Wants to Be a Millionaire* in between, and worst of all, the holy
of holies, you can't fuck anyone else on pain of marital and
social excommunication. If they want to live like zombies,
let them. Gay people, gay men have a more civilised and
sophisticated approach to life.

Danny   You mean like anonymous handjobs in public
toilets and group sex in dark rooms in the backs of pubs.

Terrence *brings over the drinks. He sits beside* Jude, *while*
Danny *and* **Jonah** *sit together on the other sofa.*

Terrence   It's just not realistic to expect one person to
remain faithful to another. I mean, it just doesn't work, does
it? The people who stay faithful end up sexless and
miserable, and the people who don't get found out and their
lives get turned upside down. These are the straight
community's rules and regulations. They make life so
bloody boring and they don't even work. Far better to adopt
a more modern approach.

Jonah   Let's not get on to this.

Danny   Like?

Terrence   Well . . . / . . .

Jonah   I said let's not get on to this.

Terrence   Did you? An arrangement.

Jude   An open relationship?

Terrence   An open relationship. You can sleep with other people if you want to. You can do it with your partner, threesomes, foursomes, whatever. Or you can do it on your own with someone else. You keep the relationship going and you get to fuck whoever you want. Who says you can't have your cake and eat it?

Jude   And it works?

Jonah   There's only one rule. You're not allowed to start an affair.

Terrence   Other than that, everybody's happy. This is what Jonah and I have in place, and it has worked, successfully, for years. Hasn't it?

Jonah   Mm.

Danny   And no one gets hurt?

Terrence   Of course not. Sex isn't the same as love. It doesn't mean anything in and of itself. I'll show you. Jude.

Jude   What?

Terrence *gives him a long slow kiss.*

Terrence   There. Do you know what that meant? Absolutely nothing.

Danny   Isn't it the case though that one person always wants that kind of relationship more than the other, so that the other one is blackmailed into accepting it because if he doesn't he risks losing his partner completely?

Terrence   Not in our case, Dr Ruth. I can only speak for ourselves, we agreed that it was what we wanted and we have both been willing and enthusiastic participants. Only last weekend he fucked a rent boy in Brighton. He told me about it earlier – with relish.

Jonah   For God's sake, Terrence.

Terrence   What?

Jonah   I didn't sleep with anyone last weekend.

Terrence   What are you talking about? You fucked some saucy seaside rent boy.

Jonah   That's enough.

Terrence   What's the matter?

Jonah   I didn't sleep with anyone. You know I didn't.

Terrence   It's a bit late to change your story now just because the boys are here.

Jonah   Terrence, I . . . /

Terrence   There's no need to be embarrassed. You wanted it, so you did it.

Jonah   For Christ's sake Terrence I made it up!

Beat.

Terrence   What did you just say to me?

Jonah   I made it up.

Terrence   What?

Jonah   Yes.

Terrence   You're lying. Tell the truth, Jonah. Tell them you fucked that boy.

Jonah   I won't.

Terrence   You will.

Jonah   I won't.

Beat.

Terrence   You better tell them.

Beat.

Jonah   I fucked him.

There is an embarrassed silence for a few moments.

Terrence   I think it's time we all had a cheeky little line. Jude, I'll rack 'em up, you make more drinks.

He gets the drugs box from the cabinet. **Jude** *makes the drinks.*

Four big fat ones.

Terrence *does his line, then hands a note to* **Jonah**. *He does his line, offers the note to* **Danny**, *who hesitates.*

Terrence   Come on, Danny, what are you, the only DJ in London who doesn't do coke?

Danny *does his line.*

Danny   Ooph.

Jude *comes over with the drinks and then does his line.*

Danny   Good gear. Where do you get it?

Terrence   An ex of mine. It's uncut – I prefer everything that way.

Jude   I like it cut with K. You don't get so wired.

Terrence   Horse anaesthetic isn't quite my cup of tea. The last time I did some I collapsed, which was slightly embarrassing given that I was in Harvey Nicks at the time.

Jude   I had to take him to the Gucci resus' room for some oxygen and a glass of champagne. What I miss is a really good E. What happened to the good Es ? Everything's shit now.

Danny   Do you know what I used to do? Half an E and a quarter of a trip.

Terrence   Doesn't sound like very much.

Jude   Don't do trips – too scary.

Danny   If you only do a quarter you don't get all the scary pictures and lights and stuff. You just get really fucking high and very, very giggly, it's brilliant.

Jude   I used to get so fucking horny on a good E. I could keep going all day and all night.

Danny   I'll get some. (*To* **Jude**.) Ever had Viagra?

Beat.

Terrence (*to everyone*)   What's the craziest sex you ever had on drugs?

Jonah   Do you remember that weekend we had in Edinburgh?

Terrence   Not between us. I don't want to talk about us. I mean with somebody else. Come on, Jonah.

Jonah   There was this Oriental guy I met once . . .

Terrence   I didn't know you were a rice queen.

Jonah   Do you want to know the rest?

Terrence   Yes.

Jonah   He took me back to his flat. In Hackney I think it was.

Terrence   Hackney!? Are you sure he wasn't a lesbian?

Jonah   He took me home, we got naked . . . /

Terrence   And then?

Jonah   He asked me to get on top of the wardrobe that was beside his bed.

Danny   What?

Terrence   MFI if he lived in Hackney.

Danny   Why?

Jonah   That's what I wondered.

Terrence   Did you get up there? I bet you did.

Jonah   Yes. He was cute. Then, he asks me to piss on him from the top of the wardrobe.

Danny   Fucking hell.

Terrence   What happened next?

Jonah   I couldn't do it at first. I think I'd had an E. I had to ask him to run a tap to help me, there was a sink in his room.

Terrence   Oh my god, it was a bed-sit.

Danny   What did he do?

Jonah   He got off on it, really got off on it, right there.

Danny   Talk about Chinese water torture.

Terrence   I think the whole thing's quite ironic.

Jonah   How is it ironic?

Terrence   Given how often you get pissed on from a great height yourself.

Terrence *laughs boisterously,* **Jude** *follows suit, and* **Danny** *too but less so.*

Jonah   What about you, Jude?

Jude   What?

Terrence   Yes, what's yours, Judey?

Jude   What?

Jonah   What's your story, come on, you *must* have a story.

Beat.

Jude   I have a story.

Terrence   Good.

Jude   It was a year ago. I was in Rupert Street, the bar. This guy, good-looking, had been eyeing me up. There was something about him, he was a little older than me but I've never cared about that. He came over, we got chatting, it turns out he's an important man, not famous, let's say he has a lot going for him. He wants to fuck me but he can't take me home because he lives with someone. We get into a cab and he takes me to Number One Aldwych, which in case you didn't know is the best hotel in London. He gets a suite, champagne, then he brings out the coke. We do all the coke, and we do everything. We fuck on the bed, on the floor, in the bath, everywhere *but* on top of the wardrobe. He put coke on the tip of my dick, which was amazing, he was rimming me – taking a drink of champagne and squirting it up my arse. Other things. It's the best fucking sex I've ever had. We wake up in the morning, have sex again of course, a champagne breakfast, then he has to go. He kisses me goodbye and gives me his number. I used it.

Beat.

Terrence   I don't think I can top that.

Jonah   Tell them about one of our nights together.

Terrence   That's private.

Jonah   So what?

Terrence   It wouldn't top Jude's story. Danny, I am dying to hear from you.

Danny   I can't think of anything.

Jude   You must have something.

Terrence   Come on, Danny.

Jude   Come on.

Beat.

Danny   I've got one. So, I'm getting this great blow job . . . /

Jude   Sounds good so far.

Terrence   Ssh.

Danny   And I'm having a threesome, did I mention that?

Terrence   No, but please go on.

Danny   The guy in front of me is sucking me off, the other one's behind me, he's going to fuck me. I feel this thing moving around next to my arsehole, it's not fingers, not a dick, something else. I'm wondering, what the fuck is it? It feels nice, smooth and cool, I can feel it's lubed up, I think what the hell. A few seconds later, I feel it going inside me, it feels great, up and down, in and out – you know. So, the blow-job's getting faster and faster, so is this thing going in and out of me, I can feel myself building, building, I know I'm going to explode, I'm going fucking crazy and I'm moaning, moaning like fuck, it starts, I can feel it, I can feel I'm going to come, then – I completely let go, my head is spinning, I come and come. I catch my breath, I'm thinking what was that thing, I look down behind me, there it is.

Jude   What?

Danny   A dildo – in the shape of the Pope, with a pointy hat.

They start laughing.

Terrence   No fucking way.

Danny   All I could think was, what would my priest say?

Jude   'Where can you buy one?' probably.

Danny   I've been a pro-lapsed Catholic ever since.

Jude   That wasn't true.

Danny   Every last word. Hand up to God. The best blow job I ever had – bar none.

Terrence   Not even Kate?

Beat.

Jude   Kate? You said Kate.

Terrence   Yes, Kate.

Beat.

Jude   What's going on? Danny!?

Terrence   Sorry, did I say the wrong thing?

Beat.

Danny   Kate was my lover.

Jude   What?

Danny   We went out together. It didn't work out – obviously.

Jude   How long?

Danny   What?

Jude   How long?

Danny   Two years. I'll tell you all about it some other time, not now, not here.

Jude   Two years!?

Danny   I know, that's a lifetime in gay years.

Jude   Why haven't you told me?

Danny   Because I knew this would happen.

Jude   What does that mean? I've told you everything about me.

Danny   Have you? Kate and I are mates, she's a really good friend.

Jude   And that's all?

Danny   You want to know if I'm still fucking her. Ask me. Come on. Ask me!

Jude   Are you?

Danny   I am so sick of this bullshit. You think I'm like you, like all of you? Fuck it. Fuck you! I'm out of here.

*Danny exits, **Jude** goes after him.*

Jude   Wait. Danny. Danny!

*We hear the front door slam. **Jude** re-enters.*

Terrence.

Terrence   It's okay, Jude.

Jude   What's going on?

Terrence   It's going to be okay.

***Jude**, upset, tries to break away, **Terrence** holds on to him.*

Jude   I have to catch up with him.

Terrence   You can't go after him.

Jude   I've got to.

Terrence   He's still mad at you. Let him cool off, he'll come back.

Jude   What if he doesn't, I'm going after him.

Terrence   Come now, Jude.

Jude   No!

Terrence   Jonah will get him then.

Jonah   I'm sorry?

Terrence   Jonah, please. Calm him down and bring him back.

Jonah   Why not let him come back when he's ready, Terrence?

Jude   I'll get him.

Terrence   No. Jonah, for God's sake, stop arguing and get on with it. Go on.

Jonah *exits*.

Terrence   Come on now. No one's been upset at Jonah leaving the room for years. Shall I make us a cup of tea?

Jude   Stay here.

Terrence   Would you like another drink?

Jude   In a minute.

Terrence   What a huge queeny drama! What a temper that Danny has. He's very butch when he's angry, isn't he? 'I'm out of here!' And what was he doing with that Kate? I just couldn't do fish. Now, what are you getting yourself into such a state for?

Jude   I'm afraid.

Terrence   Why?

Jude   Why hasn't he told me?

Terrence   I don't know.

Jude   Don't you think he should have told me?

Terrence   I would have been surprised if he had told you.

Beat.

Jude   How did you know?

Terrence   I don't want to get involved.

Jude   What is it?

Terrence   I can't.

Jude   What is it, Terrence?

Beat.

Terrence   He told me about her earlier.

Jude What?

Terrence He's still fucking her.

Jude That's not true.

Terrence That's what he told me.

Jude How? Why?

Terrence We had a chat. We decided to lay our cards on the table.

Jude You're lying.

Terrence How else could I know? He knew about you and me, I just confirmed it for him. I think he told me about Kate because he wanted to save face. You asked.

Jude Yes.

Terrence Don't be fooled by the temper tantrum. He's been fucking her the whole time he's been seeing you.

Jude He just said it was over.

Terrence You think he's different, don't you? You think he's better than the rest of us. He isn't. He's nothing but a rude little working class prick who's trying to make a few bob. I tell you what, I'll be counting the cutlery before I go to bed tonight.

Jude Oh for God's sake Terrence.

Terrence He probably thinks you've got money. Little does he know you've got sweet f.a.

Jude Thanks.

Terrence Oh I didn't mean it like that. I'm just trying to look out for you Jude. Haven't I always looked out for you? Haven't I? Well?

Jude Yes.

Terrence And I still want to Jude. You know I do.

Beat.

Jude   I've only got your word. About him and Kate.
You've got no proof. I just . . . no, Danny is different, he's
not like you, if he says it's over, I believe him.

Terrence   You need proof?

Beat.

Terrence   All right – I'll prove it.

Jude   How? It's your word against his.

Terrence   There's a way.

Jude   What way?

Terrence   I'll fuck the little bastard myself – then you'll
know what he really is.

Jude   No.

Terrence   You trust him, don't you?

Jude   This is not right.

Terrence   But you want to know. If he's the one, you
have to know.

Jude   You'll offer him money.

Terrence   What difference whether he's bought or
seduced?

Beat.

Jude   He won't do it.

Terrence   Won't he?

Beat.

Jude   One thing. If he won't, you and I are finished.

Terrence   What?

Jude   I mean it.

Terrence   You're not serious.

Jude   I am.

Beat.

Do you want a drink?

Terrence   Yes.

Jude *makes drinks for them both.*

Jude   You're going to quite extraordinary lengths to get rid of this one. Let's hope Jonah brings him back.

Terrence   He will. You know Jonah.

Beat.

Jude   They may not be back for a while.

Terrence   So?

Jude   This may be our last time alone.

Terrence   It won't be.

Beat.

Jude   Why don't we go upstairs?

Terrence   What?

Jude   Why not?

Terrence   What if they come back?

Jude   It could be our last time together Terrence. I want to say goodbye, properly. We've never done it in your bed before. We'll hear them if they come in. We can make something up.

Terrence *and* **Jude** *exit together.*

Blackout.

Act Two

Scene One

On the rise, **Danny** *is sitting down.* **Jonah** *is at the drinks cabinet.*

Danny   Where the fuck are they?

Jonah   No idea.

Danny   Jude probably thought I wasn't coming back and went clubbing.

Jonah   I'm sure they won't be long. Terrence can't stay out late these days, what with his double incontinence.

Jonah *passes him a drink.*

Danny   Thanks.

Jonah   You're welcome.

Danny   For coming to get me.

Jonah   That's okay.

Beat.

Danny   You okay?

Jonah   You were right, earlier on. You said about one person wanting to fuck around more than the other. I've never wanted that.

Danny   You guys have had ten years together. That's something.

Jonah   Ten years. I had such confidence in us then. When I met him, forget all that 'head' waiter business. He was in love with me. He's embarrassed by that now. We did ordinary things together, we didn't need the clubs and bars any more because we'd found each other, shopping, restaurants, holidays, dinner parties, the things that people do. We were happy. Then inevitably, I suppose, he suggested why don't we go out on the scene for a night. I thought why not, it'll be a change, a laugh, we hadn't been out like that for years. I know how dreadful the scene is, so does Terrence, we're not stupid. I thought, one look again at what's out there will be enough. It was for me. The scene is so addictive, you get such a rush when you go back out there, all the boys looking at you, looking to pick up, they don't care that you're in a couple, it doesn't matter that you're with your lover, they don't respect that, they still flirt with you, they still chat you up – they just don't give a fuck. Terrence wanted to take someone home with us that night. I said no. He did him in the toilets. Other times since, he's gone out with me and left me in a club while he's gone home with someone else. If you leave it a few years, there's all these new guys, guys you've never seen before, fresh meat. It'll always be there won't it, trying to pull you back in. I'd like to firebomb the whole cheap soulless fucking thing.

Danny   He's still with you.

Jonah   Look at us. We don't fuck any more, not each other. He'd like to sack me and start again. He gets offers, albeit they're from guys who want his money more than they want him. He feels he's too old to start again, he'd be taking too much of a chance. He knows I'll always love him and stay with him.

Danny   Maybe he still loves you.

Jonah   Maybe.

Danny   Have you thought about getting out? It's not my place to say, I know, but you could meet someone else.

Jonah   I don't want someone else. I want him to love me as much as I love him, to need me again the way he did when we first met. I'd give anything to get that back.

Beat.

You don't think much of Terrence and me, do you?

Danny   I know you have to compromise in relationships. If you compromise too much you lose sight of why you're there.

Beat.

Jonah   And Jude?

Danny   Jude's in love with me. He told me so.

Jonah   Good for you.

Danny   There's a problem. He's having an affair, someone who's already in a relationship. He told me about it, he didn't have to, but he did. I want him to finish it. It's hard for him, he's only been seeing me for a month, this other guy a lot longer. I'm better for him.

Jonah   Yes. One can let things go too far sometimes.

Danny   I think so.

Jonah   I think so too. (*Finishes his drink.*) Do you want another?

Danny   No thanks.

Jonah   I'm going to have one.

The front door is heard opening and closing. **Jude** *and* **Terrence** *enter, flustered.*

Jude   Hi. You came back. We went to look for you. You okay?

Danny   Yes. You?

Jude   Yes. It looked like it was going to rain, we ran back. I'm sorry. About the Kate thing. It was stupid.

Danny   You can trust me.

Jude   I do, Danny. It's me that needs work.

They kiss.

Terrence (*to* **Jude**)   Get me a drink will you, darling.

Jude *moves to drinks cabinet.* **Terrence** *sits beside* **Danny**.

Terrence (*to* **Jonah**)   How are you?

Jonah   Same as usual.

Terrence   Great. (*Then, meaning his getting* **Danny** *back to the house*) Good job.

Jude *comes over with the drinks, sits beside* **Jonah**.

Terrence   Jude and I were discussing holidays.

Jonah   Where were you thinking of going?

Terrence   Not us, you idiot. You and me.

Jonah   Where are we off to this time?

Terrence   I thought – Ibiza.

Jonah   Again?

Danny   I thought you'd be more of a Morocco man, or Thailand.

Terrence   Danny, those nails of yours are starting to show.

Jonah   We've been there.

Danny   Which one?

Jonah   Both.

Terrence   What do you think?

Jonah   If you like.

Terrence   Don't gush too much. It'd be wonderful, was last time. Great restaurants, lovely little bars, the clubs obviously, the beaches . . .

Jonah   . . . the boys.

Terrence   What's the name of that gay beach?

Jonah   Es Cavallet.

Terrence Yes.

Danny There's a gay beach?

Terrence Haven't you been? Es Cavallet. All the gay boys parading up and down, there's a little café/bar at one end, at the other there's some sand dunes and bushes – all sorts of nonsense going on in there. And let's not forget the best bit.

Jonah It's a nudist beach.

Terrence It's optional, but it's an option many of the gay boys take up, particularly the well-endowed ones. Yes, I've met some very nice people on Ibiza. The old town is lovely, the castle and everything. And you can get fabulous clothes there too. Many of the top designers have shops there now. Yes there's lots of money there. And that's where the gay boys are! Then you have San Antonio on the other side of the island, which is sort of the Blackpool of the island. Most of the straight people are there. It's all rather cheap lager, and egg 'n' chips, and 'd'you fancy a shag doggy-style darlin' and all that. Lots of people from 'up north' seem to like it. When were we last there? Was it two or three years ago?

Jonah I don't remember.

Terrence It was three. We'd just sold the flat in St John's wood, made two fifty on that. We went out to celebrate. (*To* **Danny**.) You've never been?

Danny I'm going in September, check out the clubs and the music, network, meet the DJs, the club owners. I want to get a gig out there next year.

Terrence You're quite the hustler, aren't you?

Danny Nobody's going to do it for me.

Terrence Mm. I enjoy the clubs, the music's not completely my cup of tea.

Danny What do you like?

Terrence You wouldn't approve.

Danny Try me.

Jonah Judy Garland meets Julie Andrews meets Barbara
Streisand meets Shirley Bassey . . .

Danny A diva queen?

Terrence Shamelessly. Bet you can't guess my favourite
actress?

Jonah Elizabeth Taylor.

Danny At least I know I don't have to guess who your
favourite princess was.

Terrence Taking the piss?

Danny Famous, glamorous yet unhappy women whose
tragic experiences with men mirror the gay man's own sad
experience of unrequited love and unsuccessful
relationships. But they fight on through the pain, heroines to
the end.

Terrence What about Madonna then? Even you must
like Madonna.

Danny Must I? I do like Madonna.

Terrence My God, a concession.

Danny Because her music is cool.

Terrence I'll take whatever I can get.

Terrence *looks at* **Jude**.

Jude Danny, we should go, it's getting late.

Terrence Don't be ridiculous, it's not even eleven yet.

Danny Whatever.

Terrence Come on, boys, call yourselves queens? This
won't do. How about some more lines?

Jude I'm tired.

Terrence   Then you need a line. We're out. Jonah, can you pop over to Jamie's for me, sweetheart?

Jonah *gives him a look.* **Terrence** *lifts the phone and starts dialling.*

Terrence   You know he never lets me away if I go. It's only round the corner. Jude will keep you company, won't you? (*To the telephone.*) Jamie? Hi, it's Terrence . . . well, and you . . . good . . . yes, I need a couple, Jonah's coming round . . . excellent . . . oh, and he's bringing a friend of ours with him, Jude . . . yes, that's right, the pretty one . . . what . . . yes . . . yes, I'm sure they would love to try it . . . yes, see you soon . . . yes . . . bye.

He puts the phone down. Beat.

Off you go. Danny and I will hold the fort. (*To* **Jonah**.) Cash.

He gets out his wallet and gives **Jonah** *money.*

He says he's got some new grass he wants you to try. From India.

Jonah   Which means we'll be there for ever.

Terrence   Just have one spliff, keep him happy. So, see you in about half an hour?

Jude (*to* **Danny**)   See you later.

Danny   Have fun.

Jonah *and* **Jude** *exit.* **Jude** *re-enters.*

Terrence   Forget something?

Jude *exits. The front door opens and closes. Beat.*

Terrence   Well.

Danny   Well?

Terrence   Shall we do another cheeky one?

Danny   I thought you were all out.

Terrence   I keep a small emergency supply, just in case.

Danny   You're terrible, Terrence.

Terrence   You have no idea.

He gets the drugs box, racks up two lines.

This stuff is great.

Danny   Can't argue with that.

Terrence   We're making progress already. Your line.

They do their lines.

Danny   It is nice, isn't it?

Beat.

Terrence   You were right, earlier on.

Danny   About what?

Terrence   You and I are alike.

Danny   I was joking. We have nothing in common.

Terrence   We have at least one thing in common. You remind me of me when I was a young gay man.

Danny   I come from somewhere completely different from you, a place you could never understand.

Terrence   I'm not talking about our backgrounds.

Danny   What then?

Terrence   When you look at me, what do you see?

Danny   Do you really want me to answer that?

Terrence   When I was your age, I was a lot like you. Full of self-belief, uncompromising, ambitious, cute. You had to be tough to be a gay man then.

Danny   That so?

Terrence　That was before Stonewall, you've heard of Stonewall?

Danny　The riots in New York.

Terrence　We didn't quite make those headlines over here, but gay men in London, I was one, decided that we wanted to do something too, to make a statement, to change things, to stop hiding and get out there and let people know that we were here. Britain's first gay march, 150 of us traipsing across Highbury Fields. It was a fucking beautiful day, Danny, it had rained early in the morning so it was still a little muddy, a few dykes turned up in wellies, nothing's changed, eh? We walked, men with long hair held hands and kissed. We had a picnic in the afternoon, so innocent. There was just this light in everyone's eyes, it was as if we'd started a new religion, and we were true believers. Doesn't sound like much now, it was heady stuff, a defining moment. It was the beginning of our liberation. We already had our freedom, now we were discovering our identity as gay men. We came together and suddenly we had power. We could do whatever we wanted now, and it felt like nobody and nothing could touch us any more.

Danny　Freedom and liberation – for what? What's liberating about all looking the same, all liking the same music, all speaking the same way – is that an identity?

Terrence　I understand.

Danny　Do you?

Terrence　Things are changing.

Danny　Not fast enough.

Terrence　You've got time on your side.

Danny　You don't need time. You have Jonah.

Beat.

Terrence　I'm not in love with Jonah. I don't want to be on my own either. Can you really see me out there looking for love again at fifty? Do you think I want to be doing that all over again?

Danny   You are. What are you fucking doing with Jude?

Terrence   I care about him.

Danny   So dump Jonah and take your chances.

Terrence   It's not that simple.

Danny   You're scared.

Terrence   No.

Danny   You might be able to hang on to Jude for a while, you know you could never keep him. I could.

Terrence   A confident man – because he told you he was in love with you, once. Sometimes that's just something you say.

Danny   I've never said it.

Terrence   Who was fucking who at the time?

Danny   It wasn't like that. Has he ever said it to you – even if he didn't mean it?

Beat.

Terrence   You're something, aren't you, kiddo?

Danny   Give it up.

Terrence   You want him? How much?

Danny   What?

Terrence   How much?

Danny   I want him for the right reasons, that's enough.

Beat.

Terrence   What would you be prepared to do, to get him?

Danny   What do you mean?

Terrence If you want him, you can have him. I'll give him up. I'm serious. But there's a condition. I'm not going to give him up for nothing, am I?

Danny Cut to the chase.

Beat.

Terrence Fuck me. If you fuck me, you can have him.

Danny I'd rather fuck your mother.

Terrence That's my offer.

Danny No.

Terrence Take it or leave it.

Danny Leave it.

Terrence Then I'm going to take him off you.

Danny You can't.

Terrence Yes I can.

Beat.

Danny Why me?

Terrence Because I haven't. Because I've wanted to get my dick inside you from the moment you came in here tonight.

Danny No.

Terrence You won't get another chance. If you want him, this is it.

Danny I don't trust you.

Terrence Danny, you have to trust me.

Beat.

Do it, or I'll have Jude in here within a week!

Danny You're fucking evil.

Pause.

Okay.

Terrence   Good boy.

Terrence *moves to the door.*

Danny   Where are you going?

Terrence   Upstairs.

Danny   No. Here.

They go behind the sofas. **Danny** *makes* **Terrence** *start sucking him.* **Terrence** *flips him over the sofa as if to start fucking him, starts trying to remove* **Danny**'s *trousers.* **Danny** *stops him.*

Danny   No. I want my big fucking dick inside you, Terrence.

They switch positions, go at it again, they undo **Terrence**'s *pants, he is put over the sofa.* **Danny** *spits on to his hands, slaps it on to* **Terrence**'s *arsehole and on to his own penis. He starts to fuck him.*

Terrence   Stop!

Danny   Is it hurting?

Terrence   Yes.

Danny *carries on until he almost comes, then pulls out.*

Terrence   Did you come?

Danny   No. I can't. I don't want to.

Terrence   Get back in there and finish it you little cunt!

Danny *looks at him, moves him roughly back around. He goes back in, giving it everything, comes. He is crying. He does up his trousers and sits.* **Terrence** *does up his trousers and sits on the other sofa.*

Terrence   Was I that bad?

Beat.

What's wrong with you?

Blackout.

Scene Two

Terrence *is sitting on his own, smoking a cigarette, thinking. A few moments pass . . .*

Terrence   Enough.

. . . and he puts the cigarette out. The front door opens and closes. **Jude** *enters.*

Jude   Where is he?

Terrence   Upstairs.

Jude *looks at* **Terrence** *who smiles and nods.* **Jonah** *enters, oblivious to this, starts making himself a drink.*

Jonah   Well he's doing all right isn't he, he's had his place done up *again*, God knows how much he spent this time, and he's got two young guys round there, what some people will do for coke I don't know, and as for that grass, well I wasn't going to touch any of it, stuck up his arse for twelve hours it was when he flew back from India a couple of weeks ago, I'm not sure whether it smelled that foul before he put it up there but I wasn't going to take any chances, anyway I never thought we were going to get away, that Jamie never shuts up, he does talk the most awful shit, I think he takes too many of his own drugs. People talk such bollocks on drugs. Where's Danny?

Terrence   Upstairs.

Jonah   Is he okay?

Terrence   Go and see.

Jonah *exits.*

Terrence   It's okay.

Jude   No.

Terrence   It's okay.

Jude   I don't believe you.

Terrence   Look at me. I fucked him.

Jude   No!

Terrence   I fucked him, then I told him why I fucked him. Just in case you changed your mind. He wouldn't take you gift-wrapped now.

Jude   You didn't.

Terrence   Forget him.

Beat.

I have something to tell you.

Jude   What?

Terrence   I'm going to ask Jonah to leave tonight. I want you to move in.

Jude   Are you serious?

Terrence   I won't wait around any more and take the chance of you ending up with someone else.

Beat.

Jude   This is a surprise.

Terrence   This isn't a game any more, Jude. This is about the rest of my life.

Jude *does not reply.*

Terrence   I thought this was what you wanted?

Jude   Yes, but . . . /

Terrence   But what?

Beat.

Jude   I'll need space if this is going to work. You understand.

Terrence   Of course I understand.

Jude   It'll work both ways. If you want to/

Terrence   I know how it works. And Danny?

Jude   What about him?

Terrence   You can't see him again.

Jude   You said he'd never want to see me again anyway.

Terrence   I'm talking about you now, what I need from you.

Jude   I don't know if I can promise that.

Terrence   You better be very fucking careful, Jude, because you could walk out of here tonight with nothing.

Jude   But Danny /

Terrence   No! No more Danny. Make up your mind.

Beat.

Jude   All right.

Beat.

Terrence *kisses him.*

Jude   But where would Jonah go, what would he do?

Terrence   Leave that to me.

Jonah *enters.*

Jonah   He's just coming. He was taking a shower.

Beat.

Jonah   I know what we need.

He exits and returns with a bottle of champagne and four champagne flutes, all on a tray, which he puts down on the table.

Tarrraaah!

He begins to open the champagne and sees that no one is reacting to him.

(*Waving at the others to sit down.*) Come on.

Terrence *sits beside* **Jonah**. **Danny** *enters and sits beside* **Jude**.

Jonah   Good. Everything in its proper place.

He pops the champagne, pours glasses for them all and hands them round.

What is the matter?

Terrence   Jonah, there's something I have to tell you.

Jonah   Terrence, can't it wait? We have guests.

Beat.

Terrence   It's over. Us – we're finished.

No response.

Did you hear me?

Jonah   I heard you.

Terrence   It's best if you leave tonight, pack some things and go. I'll send on the rest later. Jude is moving in. I don't want to waste any more time.

Jonah   Jude?

Terrence   Jude.

Jonah   I don't understand.

Terrence   Yes you do.

Beat.

Jonah   Yes I do.

Terrence   If you can't fight for what you want in this business, you have to get out. You never had the guts to fight for me, Jonah.

Jonah   I was afraid I'd lose you. I love you.

Terrence   Not good enough.

Beat.

Jonah You cunt.

Jonah *exits*.

Terrence I won't be long.

Terrence *exits*.

Danny That's it.

Jude Yes.

Danny Why? Because I fucked that old prick?

Jude Don't call him that.

Danny I asked you a question. Because I fucked him?

Jude Yes.

Danny So what? You fuck him all the time.

Jude That's different. Why?

Danny I had reasons.

Beat.

Jude I needed to know.

Danny You're a fucking fool. When you're in love with someone, you don't test it, you don't play games with it, you grab it and you keep it and you kick the shit out of anyone who tries to take it off you. He told me if I had sex with him, he'd let you go.

Jude He didn't say that.

Danny He did. Want to change your mind?

Jude I'm sorry.

Danny You're like a kid. You think you can say sorry and it's all forgotten. I want something better too, I thought you were it, I was wrong, but that's okay.

Terrence *enters*.

Terrence Jonah is packing. Are we all sorted out? I'll make some drinks.

Jude *and* **Danny** *sit down on opposite sofas.*

Jude Where is he going?

Terrence Not feeling guilty, I hope, darling. Don't. I don't. He has a sister in Bayswater. I think she has a little flat over there. He'll be fine. I've given him a cheque to tide him over, until he finds another job.

Jude What?

Terrence I can't keep him on.

Jude Why not?

Terrence It wouldn't be appropriate. He thinks so too. He'll find something else.

He comes over with the drinks.

(*To* **Danny**) There we are.

He sits down beside **Jude**.

Jude I should be going soon.

Terrence No reason for you to go. Jonah will be leaving soon. You might as well stay the night.

Beat.

What?

Jude My things are at Danny's. I was going to be staying there tonight.

Terrence Well, when Danny goes I can book him a cab on the account, and it can brings back your things after it drops him off. You don't mind, do you, Danny?

Danny Why would I?

Terrence So that's it.

Jude Yes.

Beat.

Danny   No.

Terrence   What?

Danny   I'm not finished.

Terrence   If you intend starting a slanging match,
Danny, you should go. Nothing you say is going to make
any difference. You lost.

Danny   How many of us have you had? How many guys
have you fucked and not given a fuck about? How many do
you actually remember? You're going to remember me.
You're just like him, Terrence, my first lover, my old guy –
all you fucking faggots are. I'd never been fucked before, I
wanted the first time to be special, to be with someone
special, to be something I would remember for the rest of
my life. I let him fuck me. He used me. Left me still bleeding
and fucked off.

Jonah *enters.*

Terrence   Is there a point?

Danny   I didn't make you take it for fun, Terrence.

Terrence   What do you mean?

Danny   From him, to me, to you. Do you see the beauty
of it?

Terrence   What?

Danny   I never deserved it. But you really fucking do.

Terrence *looks at* **Jude**.

Jude   I don't know anything about it.

Terrence   Come on, Danny. You're frightening the kid.

Danny   I never told him because we never fucked.

Beat.

Terrence   You're lying.

Danny   No.

Beat.

Jude   Did *he* fuck *you*?

Terrence   What?

Jude   Did he?

No response.

Did he wear a condom?

Terrence   Of course not. It just happened.

Jude   My God.

Terrence   It's all right, Jude. It's simply a lie.

Danny   You're pretty cool under fire, aren't you, Terrence? I suppose that's why your lot always made such great officers when we had the empire. Twenty thousand screaming savages bearing down on you, held off with only six men and your service revolver. It won't do you any good. It can't. I'm telling the truth.

Terrence   Prove it.

Danny   How would you like me to do that? Cut my wrists open and see if the blood burns a hole in your expensive fucking carpet?

Terrence   You can't, can you, because it's not true. Get out.

Danny *takes out a pill box from his pocket and throws it at* **Terrence**.

Terrence   What's this?

Terrence *opens it.*

Danny   Delavirdine. D4Ts. DDIs.

Beat.

Terrence   So what!? Lots of people do it and don't get it.

Danny   It hurt. You remember?

Terrence   And?

Danny   When I pulled out, there was blood on my dick. From you, from your arse. You were bleeding when I came inside you.

Beat.

Terrence   Jude, why don't you say something?

Jude (*to* **Danny**)   You said I'm okay.

Danny   What?

Jude   I'm okay?

Danny   Yes.

Beat.

Terrence   Jude.

No response

Terrence   I love you.

No response

Terrence   It'll be all right.

No response

Terrence   Jude!

Jude   What?

Terrence   Are you okay?

Jude   I'm okay.

Terrence   I need you, Jude.

Beat.

Jude   I should go.

Terrence   Jude!

Jude   What!?

Terrence   I love you.

Jude   I have to go.

Jude *gets up to go.*

Terrence   Please. Jude. Stay with me.

Jude *moves to go.*

Terrence   Jude! Please! I can't do this on my own! For fuck's sake!

Jude *stops.*

Terrence   I'll give you anything you want.

Jude   I don't want what you have to give.

Jude *exits.*

Terrence   Jude.

The front door opens and closes. **Danny** *moves to* **Terrence**.

Danny   Game over.

Jonah   You should go.

Danny   So should you.

Danny *exits. Pause.*

Jonah   I could stay tonight. If you want.

Terrence   I would like that.

Jonah   Would you?

Terrence   I'm frightened.

Jonah   I know.

Terrence   I can't do this by myself.

Jonah   You don't have to.

Terrence   Will you stay?

Jonah   Yes.

Terrence   I need you.

Jonah   I'm here. You're safe. I love you.

Terrence   Yes.

Jonah   I won't let you do this by yourself.

Terrence   Thank you.

Jonah   Are you okay?

Terrence   I'll be all right in a minute.

Pause.

Jonah   Terrence . . .

Terrence   What Jonah?

Beat.

They kiss. Fade to black.